A Niche in a Niche Industry

Beyond the Instructions

A handyman's *DREAM!*

I0439240

By
Mike Mehrle

Professional Technician & Founder
of the United Assemblers Network (UAN)

UNITED

ASSEMBLERS

Second Edition
2015

A Niche in a Niche Industry

Beyond the Instructions

A handyman's *DREAM!*

The ultimate primer for doing it right, when it comes time for assembly, installation and repair of RTA (ready to assemble) products.

ISBN-13:
978-1494974541

ISBN-10:
1494974541

Forward

If you're a handyman and are not stuck thinking that what you do has to be everything to be successful, this book is for you.

As a handyman you probably perform many tasks of skilled tradesmen such as carpenters, electricians, mechanics, plumbers, and many other trades that require some sort of training or education. Most people start a handyman service mostly because of not being trained in one of the skilled trades as mentioned; and because of that, we become skilled at many things but masters of none.

There is an unknown industry that the consumer is looking for on a regular basis. The only problem is they just don't know where to look. And the reason for that problem is that there is no organization to the industry for assembly and installation. However; that United Assemblers Network is changing the way a handyman is look at when it comes to putting things together for the public.

This is a very niche industry, and they can become even more niche by specializing in servicing one or two products that you may feel make you the most money. There are many products that require assembly and installation services; some of these products are basketball goals, playsets, furniture, fitness equipment, and then along with fitness equipment assembly installation there is repair of the fitness equipment... the list goes on and on.

As for a niche in a niche industry, you may decide that you want to specialize in installing basketball goals for example. Basketball goals can be one of the most profitable jobs in our industry along with building playsets and repairing fitness equipment. However, considering the profits for time spent and money made, basketball rolling sleighs and can be the most profitable. Once you get the experience, it should take less than four accumulated hours to complete a job and that would net you over $400 making your hourly wage a round $100 an hour...

If you don't think that you're worth $100 an hour or quite honestly more, then you probably should not be in business for yourself.

Acknowledgments

I want to thank my wife *Pattie*, (my sunshine), for providing a warm flame, as the sun always does, by giving me hope that all the work I've done will someday pay off... for everyone.

I also want to thank my mom (*Julia*) and dad (*Jack*) for buying me that erector set for Christmas back in the early 1960's. That set was the start of my interest in designing, assembling, and yes, playing in ways that developed my mechanical aptitude.

This is a very similar set I received that Christmas:

I want to thank all the customers I had over the years for trusting me to provide a service when no one else was available.

Additionally, I want to thank the manufacturers and online dealers that put their trust in me by donating products that I used to produce instructional videos for you on my YouTube channel: YouTube.com/TheSavvyTech

I say this with my deepest heartfelt gratitude in all that have been patient and made it worth my while to write this book.

THANK YOU...
Sincerely,
Your son, husband & friend... Mike

Why I wrote this book

I wanted to add these pages to help guide everyone who wants to do it right.

First, this is not a novel to read from cover to cover... *you can if you wish;* but I have developed it in such a way to be more of a reference manual than a book, although, you should read all of it to get the most out of it.

Since you bought this book, it is obvious to me that you are looking for a way to make some really good money. If that is you, you must understand that reading and understanding instructions is your most important tool. I can tell you from experience, most people don't want to read the instructions, and for those people, I seriously doubt they will read this book.

If you have a high mechanical aptitude and are looking for a very lucrative opportunity in a very niche business, the United Assemblers Network (UAN) is an awesome way to learn how to build a successful business in a tough economy... and if you do it right, it is virtually impossible to fail.

There are members of the UAN breaking six figures annually... however, they do work hard... BUT... they get to play even harder.

There is a lot of valuable information in this book that I have personally used over the years and have trained hundreds of assembly, installation and repair technicians all over the country.

To write about everything would be impossible. That's why experience is anyone's greatest teacher.

For even more information **beyond** this book on how to do it right... go to: United-Assemblers.com

Contents

Contents

There is virtually an unknown industry, that yes... requires skills!

It is becoming known as the assembly, installation & repair industry.

Why assembly is required

As you probably know, many products sold in America are not manufactured here.

Many American companies that manufacture products here are forced to provide products requiring assembly, if they want to stay in competition with the companies that have their products manufactured overseas.

Ready-to-Assemble (RTA) products require less manpower for manufacturers to produce and help reduce delivery costs. They also require less storage space for the retailer, affording lower prices for the consumer.

The "Buy American" movement will never reverse what our lifestyles have created. We need to accept the issues at hand and learn how to correctly assemble products ourselves, or know when to hire a professional.

The main problem with consumers assembling their own products is, they usually don't have the tools, time, patience or experience to do it right the first time.

But never fear, there is an unknown industry of professional product assemblers that few people know of. RTA products can be assembled by anyone, but sometimes it is better to consider hiring a professional.

Any time there is a botched assembly; the consumer considers calling the product "junk". The fact is… if it were done right the first time, that same consumer would love the RTA product and show it off to their friends and family.

Handy people and companies are rapidly appearing all across the country, claiming to be assemblers. The reason… RTA products usually have "easy assembly" written all over the boxes, so the thought is;" how hard can it really be?" The answer is for many products… not hard at all if you know what you're doing.

With the right amount of time,
patience and having the right tools...
Anyone can do it... with this book!

Who can do it?

Almost anyone should be able to assemble any product; however, many products can be too complicated for the average person, including the unexperienced technician who hasn't reached the master assembly technician level.

The average person takes up to five times longer than a seasoned professional assembler. There are guys (and gals) who can put things together; but to do it professionally, most fall short of making money at it, because they are just not accurate or fast enough.

A professional assembler is no different than a carpenter, mechanic, plumber, electrician or any other skilled tradesman.

If someone is getting paid to do the work, it's important for the consumer to feel like they're getting their money's worth. To be a professional assembler, it takes experience and knowledge to actually make money at it.

The United Assemblers Network (UAN) has a growing membership of the best independent professional assembly technicians all over the country, that provide a service that cannot be out performed by any other source, especially a National Assembly Company (NAC).

Independent technicians typically provide service for people who buy their RTA products online or through local retailers.

With the right amount of time, patience and having the right tools... Anyone can do it with a little knowledge; if this book is taken for the value it offers; afterwards, the average person will find they can put things together with more confidence.

Ultimately, to get professional results, any member from the UAN will more than likely provide the consumer the best service available in our industry. If consumers, national retailers, manufacturers and on-line dealers want to have their products assembled at a professional level, then the UAN is the only knowledgeable and organized source that can provide that service.

The best place to get started...
...open the box;
Then look for the instructions!

Getting Started

There is a box in front of you and you know the product inside is in many pieces; but never fear, the best place to get started is by opening the box and looking for the instructions.

There are multitudes of products purchased every day from local retailers and online sources all over the country; many of them will require some level of assembly.

I will be mentioning throughout this book, the need of the right tools, having enough time, practicing patience and having experience. But *always* remember, it is most important that you take the time to read the instructions.

Having the proper tools and enough time will make any assembly job go much easier; however, patience will trump tools and time, because without patience, you are susceptible to making mistakes. It would be a good idea to choose a day when you have plenty of extra time.

Many homeowners think they have all the time in the world, and for that reason, decide to take on an assembly project themselves. When the job is finished, it is very rewarding for anyone, be it the homeowner or the professional assembly technician to say, "I built that!" However, they will only say that when it is built right!

I think you should be getting the message... without enough time you will most likely become impatient and make unnecessary mistakes.

Another quality to have when it's time to assemble a product is knowledge, because without it, you will likely make bad decisions. But if you read the instructions, you should be fine.

When attempting to assemble anything, and I do mean *anything*, the first few things you should do is: clear the area you will be working in, open the box, and find the instructions.

If the instructions are not visible when you open the box, remove each part and place them so that you will be able to easily find the right parts, as they are called out in the instructions.

I have been doing this type of work for years and "still" read the instructions... it is what smart people do!

To maintain order throughout the assembly process, and to make cleanup easier, discard the packaging in trash bags as you are unpacking.

So to summarize this chapter you should make sure to do the following:

1. Clear the area
2. Have the right tools
3. Find the instructions and review them
4. Sort all of the parts out of the box, including hardware
5. Discard trash as the product is unpacked
6. Use the instructions during assembly

Finally, here is a tip to help you assemble any new product well: if possible, go to a store where the product is displayed and take lots of photos.

Take as many pictures as you can.

Take pictures at different angles and close-ups, in order reference them, along with the instructions, when you are assembling the product.

Tools

You can usually assemble products with basic tools; however, as time goes on, if you decide to do this for a living... experience will help you understand tools that will help you get a job done more efficiently and with more accuracy.

Additional Information

If you want professional insight, you can take the UANCT (United Network Assemblers Network Certification Test) and join us on our private Facebook group.

When taking on an assembly project... Always think safety!

Not reading the instructions...
...is pretty much a guy thing!

Getting through the instructions

If there is anything you get out of this book, this would be it...
"Always Read the Manufacturer's Instructions!"

Ten things to help make an assembly project successful:

1. Make sure you have the time needed to complete the project; and before starting, take a deep breath.
2. If you bought the product online, many times you can go to a local retailer and see the item already assembled. Take plenty of close-up pictures of what may look like a complicated part of the assembly.
3. Make sure you have all tools the instructions listed as needed for proper assembly.
4. Have a trash bag to place all protective packaging in as you unpack. This will keep your area uncluttered and organized and easier to work in.
5. If the manufacturer is saying the product requires a certain number of people... *make sure you have them* unless you are a professional with "special" tools that allow you to assemble something with less help.
6. When you open the box... what is the first thing you should do? Of course... look for the instructions.
7. Additionally, as you unpack, place parts in order as they are marked. For example: if the parts are labeled, place them in order of their sequence (a,b,c or 1,2,3). If parts are not labeled (and it does happen) place the parts so can recognize them by shape as shown in the instructions.
8. There are instructions that contain mostly graphics. DO NOT ignore any written content in these types of instructions; they are there for a reason.
9. There are instructions that contain few graphics and mostly text; this is where the photos you took at a local store come in handy.
10. If the instructions are unclear and you have questions, call the manufacturer.

If you follow the manufacturer's instructions and take the previous ten suggestions seriously, you will have fun and be very proud of the job you completed... and completed the right way.

Anyone should be able to build a product with a little understanding of the manufacturer's instructions, but everyone can mess up by not using them, even a pro.

Unfortunately, there are products that come with poor instructions. It takes skill and knowledge to "read between the lines" if the instructions are ambiguous.

One more thing to be aware of, you never know when a manufacturer will change the assembly process. When they do, you'll typically see an insert (hopefully a different color of paper) to make you aware of any design changes, or an amendment in assembly steps.

If you don't look for possible changes in the assembly process, (even if you're a pro), you might find yourself having to take something apart and put it back together again... which ultimately causes you headaches and lost time.

By using this book, you can work through poor instructions by having a better understanding of them by sorting out the pieces, and becoming familiar with the contents of the products parts as you unpack, don't forget pictures if you can get them.

The instructions were not written for you to "guess" where board "A" goes; or if the half inch (1/2") screw is used instead of the one inch (1") screw.

If you don't follow the suggestions in this book and/or don't follow the instructions supplied by the manufacturer, you will get frustrated; blame the product you're assembling, the engineers, or both.

By doing it right the first time, there is nothing more rewarding than having assembled something correctly where you can say, "I built that."

If you have a product that didn't come with instructions, chances are, you'll find them online.

To get some insight on a particular product being assembled, some manufacturers have videos on their websites, or should. You can also find some pretty good videos on YouTube. In fact I have a popular YouTube channel... **YouTube.com/TheSavvyTech**

Safety

If you get into this industry there are certain precautions that anyone should take to prevent injury on a job.

Knowing that providing our type of service requires not only skills but the correct tools to get the job done, familiarization of any tool that you may use is highly recommended before actually using it.

Need to move some fitness equipment?
It is not hard to do, if you know how to do it.

How to move already assembled RTA products
(Without instructions)

I have been talking about how important it is to read and understand the instructions, but if they are not available, at the very least try to find them online.

There are exceptions....

You may have something you bought a long time ago, that you need to move, or you have your eye on something used you want to buy; however, it needs to be taken apart and then reassembled after you move it.

There is a professionally proven method I developed to use when moving RTA products. The best part about something already assembled is, you shouldn't need instructions to put it back together if you use the simple technique described in this chapter.

I have moved products for clients for many years. Occasionally, they didn't need me to reassemble the product. Using this technique, they saw how easy it was to put it back together again, without the instructions.

So you may be thinking right now, "What is this secret technique where I don't need instructions?" It's simple, what you need to do is mark the parts before taking the product apart.

The best way to do this is to buy a couple of very important items. One of them is a roll of "WHITE" electrical tape and the other is a black permanent marker.

I used masking tape the first time I tried this technique for a customer; but the masking tape failed BIG TIME! During transit, the movers' accidently tore off the tape and smudged the writing.

The reassembly would have been nearly impossible because of the number of pieces and multiple cables that snaked all over this equipment. However, luckily... I took a lot of pictures as well.

Below are the two products I use when I need to move something that needs to be taken apart. The disk image on the right is just the label that covered the tape.

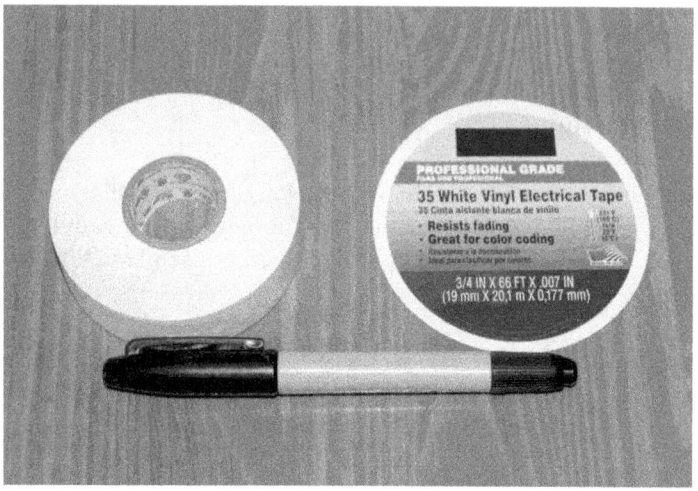

The electrical tape is nearly waterproof and will hold up to abuse, and will not tear off as easily the masking tape did. Once the marker is dry, it will stand up to abuse and any water it may encounter if the product is moved in the rain.

What you should do is pre-cut the tape as you apply it to the area that will be taken apart. Cut the pieces about 2" long, or maybe a little longer, where you might be wrapping a cable. You can always cut off excess.

Apply the tape first, and then mark the connections with identical numbers or letters or both; that way, you won't smudge the marking. Permanent markers will smudge until the ink is dry. Luckily, permanent markers dry very fast.

Place two cut pieces of tape on adjacent pieces wherever you will be taking the product apart. Create your own coding and write the same code on the two adjacent pieces of tape.

The piece of fitness equipment demonstrated here has six structural points of contact, three at the top and three at the bottom, so I began marking by using "bottom – 1", then "bottom -2" and so on. See image below:

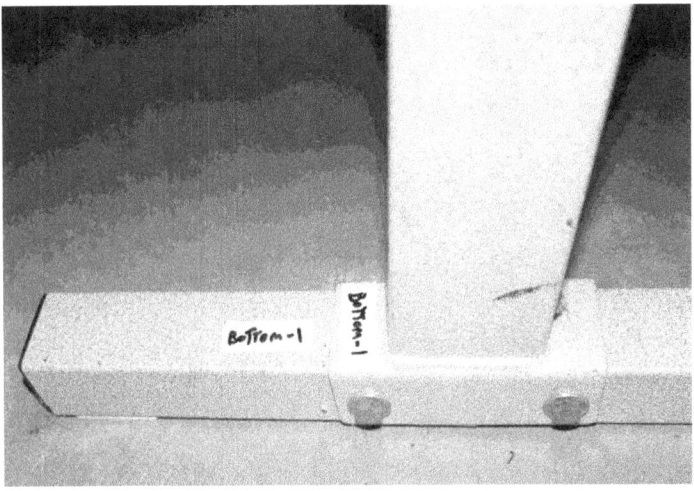

Stay consistent; as I moved up that support to the first connection (which is a seat) I marked it as "seat - 1". That way if there is another seat having holes with the same alignment, I would know which seat goes where. The more logic you use marking the parts, the easier to know what goes where later.

Marking the seat:

What do you do after everything is marked? The following photo will show you how to keep track of all the parts, placing hardware back on the pieces while they are apart.

Seat removed:

Marking the support to correctly reposition the seat:

The reason for marking the support is because there are four holes, where only two are used. As shown, under the first hole, another piece of tape is used to mark the hole where the seat is to be reassembled, since it was probably adjusted by the user in the first assembly.

Use this markup method throughout, where there is a connection with optional positioning.

As easy as it is to mark the structural pieces of the equipment... the BIGGEST headache is usually the cables and how they snake around the entire framework.

In addition to using the tape, as pointed out here, I suggest taking pictures as well, to back up the taping and marking. Take it from a professional who has done a lot of this type of work, this step is important to assure an accurate reassembly.

To make rethreading the cables easier, add some directional markings to help thread the cables correctly when it comes time to reassemble.

Note how the pulley "C-2" is marked to start the retraceable threading of the cable "C-2".

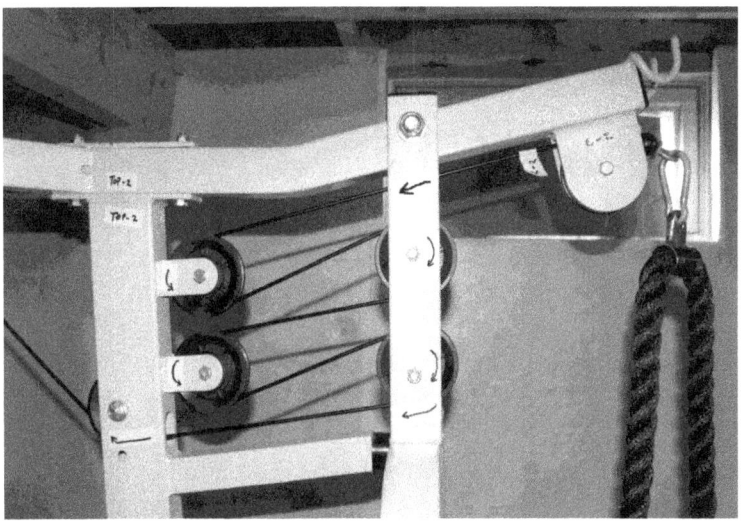

After reassembly is complete, remove all tape. A typical household cleaner should remove residue left behind from the tape. If not, you can use denatured alcohol to remove any residue.

The following are some more marked up photos...

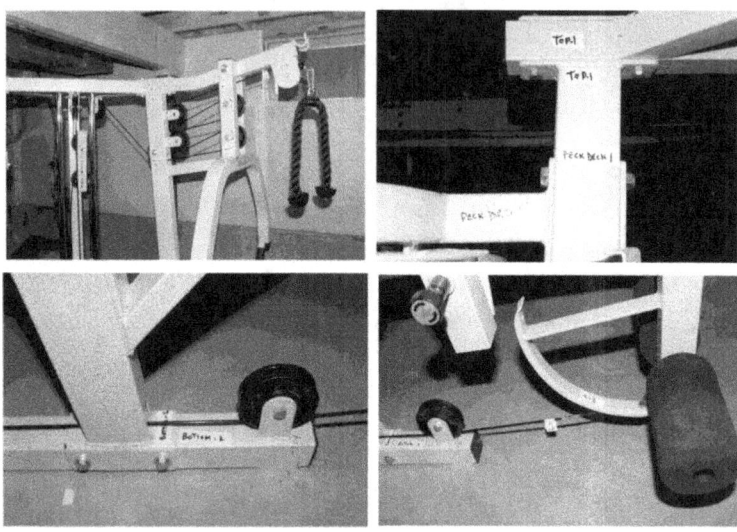

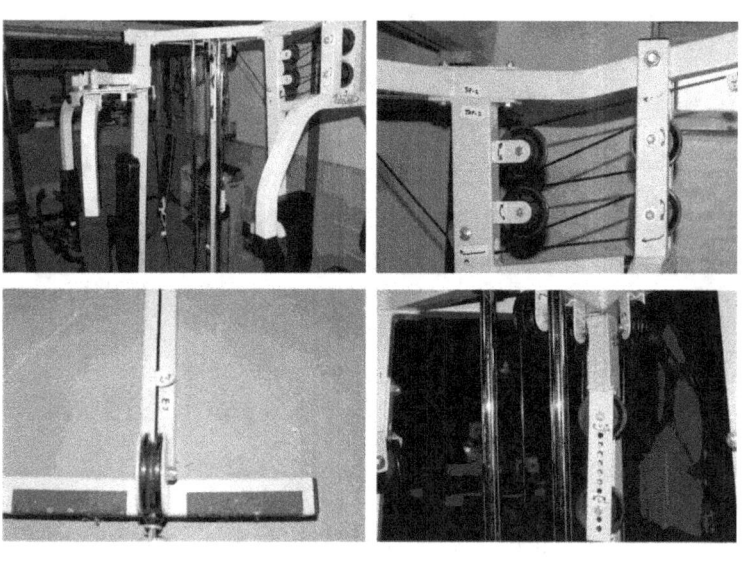

More views...

Everything you have read in this chapter can be applied to anything you need to move... furniture, play sets or anything else that can be taken apart.

If you utilize the techniques in this chapter, you should be able to put this product back together without instructions.

When taking on an assembly project...
Always think safety!

Some products requiring assembly

In the next few chapters, I will be giving basic suggestions on how to get started before each job.

It would be impossible to give detailed instructions on all products requiring assembly or installation, simply because there are so many. Besides, the manufacturer has already provided you with a set of their instructions.

By reading this book, you will develop a better understanding of what the instructions are attempting to convey, teaching you to make fewer mistakes on any given assembly project.

"*Beyond The Instructions*" primes you for properly reading the manufacturer's instructions, giving you a better understanding for use during any assembly project.

If you can follow instructions, you will have very few to maybe no problems as you conquer any assembly, installation and repair project.

If you can assemble the following products, you will most likely be able to assemble anything... that is if you follow the guidance of this book and again, the manufacturer's instructions.

- Basketball Goals

- Play Sets

- Fitness Equipment

- Furniture

Basketball Goal Installation

Basketball goals

Tools... *if you don't have the right tools and find you have to buy them just to complete the installation of a basketball goal system, consider this... you might want to hire a professional from the* **UnitedAssemblers.com**

Minimal tools needed for an in-ground installation...

Day one, digging:

- Wheelbarrow
- Spud Bar (this tool is best for digging)
- Spade shovel
- Posthole digger
- Level
- Tape Measure
- Two large crescent wrenches
- Work gloves (for digging)

Day Two, assembly (minimum four days later):

- Socket set (1/2" drive is best)
- Tape measure
- Phillips screwdriver
- Common screwdriver
- Two large crescent wrenches
- Level
- Mallet
- Optional: drill/impact driver

The following suggestion cannot be overstated... unless you have installed enough in-ground systems that you could do it in your sleep... you should always *READ THE MANUFACTURERS INSTRUCTIONS!!!*

There are many manufacturers; and the installation of each of their in-ground basketball systems are designed in different ways.

Getting to know all of the different systems and their steps to installation will take experience; however, the basics of an actual installation with all of them are basically the same.

Different type of foundations:

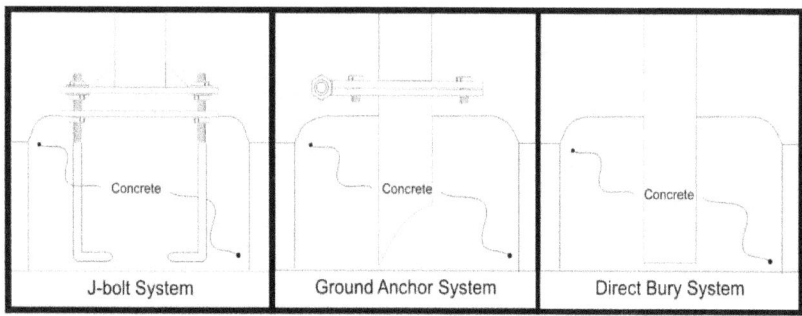

| J-bolt System | Ground Anchor System | Direct Bury System |

First day...

You need to know... Installing a basketball system "IS" a labor intensive job, digging the foundation, and then on the second day, it is dangerous standing one up.

Before you start any in-ground project, *call the utilities.* Most states have one number to call (811) that will notify most, if not all underground utilities in your area... **IT'S THE LAW THAT YOU CALL "BEFORE" YOU DIG.**

Beyond calling the 811 number, do some research and develop a plan.

Additionally, if you live in a neighborhood with a homeowners association... you better get clearance even if your neighbor already has one in the driveway. I have seen people have to either move or even remove a system because of an homeowners association.

Do you have the mechanical aptitude?

You don't need to be an engineer to install a basketball goal. It definitely helps to know where and why which tools are used when it comes time to dig the hole and completing the assembly.

IMPORTANT - The key to a successful installation, just like anything else... you MUST have a foundation that is as perfect as you can get it. The few extra minutes you spend making sure the pole, ground anchor or j-bolt system is level and plumb, will make your final assembly steps much easier, and will allow for your system to last much longer.

Digging a hole in the ground (the foundation) is typically something the average person doesn't want to do, and because of this, many people cut corners and do not dig the hole large enough.

If you don't install a proper foundation... your system will fall over... you do not want that to happen.

NOTE: "ALL" manufacturers over-engineer the foundation to cover all soil conditions around the country. Do you know the soil conditions in your area?

DO NOT cut corners as you dig the foundation, as it is outlined by the manufacturer, unless you know what you are doing.

I can't tell you how many times I have seen a goal that fell over because an inexperienced tech or homeowner that didn't dig the required foundation for the soil conditions.

"SOMETIMES"... it wouldn't hurt to install a larger foundation for places with sandy conditions.

Many people think using a spade shovel or posthole digger is the way to dig a hole. The posthole digger is actually a better tool to "clean" out a hole where the dirt has already been loosened.

The spade shovel is a good tool to dig with; but hard soil conditions will cause the person doing the digging to get frustrated, causing them to cut corners.

Start digging the hole with a spade shovel to make a clean opening. Once you are four to six inches deep, the absolute best tool to dig the rest of the hole with is a spud bar. You can drive a spud bar three to four inches into the ground each time you plunge it into the area you are digging.

What you will do: plunge the spud bar into the ground around the perimeter of the hole, then carefully pull or push the bar to break up the soil then clean it out with a posthole digger. If you do this... even the toughest soil conditions can be dug out in under a couple of hours.

VERY IMPORTANT - Before you start digging the hole and mixing concrete, <u>make sure that you have everything you need</u>, to finish all the steps required on the first day's installation of the foundation.

After the foundation is in, you need to *wait at least four days*, to allow the concrete to harden enough to stand your goal.

Second day...

Unlike digging the foundation, raising a backboard is DANGEROUS!!!

Some backboards can weigh as much as 200 pounds for consumer systems and as much as 275 pounds for institutional systems.

The consideration for the weight of a backboard is why a professional will use a crane to raise the backboard.

If you have helpers holding a heavy backboard in place, while you're reading instructions, you stand a pretty good chance of one of them possibly dropping that backboard and someone getting hurt. **Don't start assembly until ready!** Safety should always be a priority.

Make sure you have the right tools as called out earlier; and enough help to raise the backboard safely.

Most basketball systems have nuts and bolts that are very close in size, so you should measure each piece and make sure you know which hardware goes where before using them.

For a more finished look, if you are installing a system in a driveway, make sure the heads of the bolts are on the street side of the goal as you insert that hardware.

Like everything else... read the manufacturer's instructions as you assemble your goal.

UnitedAssemblers.com

Play Sets

Play Sets

Even though manufacturers will label the assembly of a play set as an easy assembly, *many of them are actually a construction project*.

Tools... *if you don't have the right tools and find you have to buy them just to complete the assembly of a play set, consider this... you might want to hire a professional.*

UnitedAssemblers.com

Minimal tools needed for a play set assembly only:

- Ladder
- Hammer
- Drill (regular & impact)
- Assortment of bits (Star, Square, Common & Phillips)
- Socket set
- Screwdrivers (Phillips & Common)
- 4 foot Level
- Line level

The following suggestion cannot be overstated... *unless you have assembled enough play sets that you could do it in your sleep... you should always READ THE MANUFACTURERS INSTRUCTIONS!!!*

There are many manufacturers of play sets, and the installation of each is basically the same.

Play set ground leveling... (Tipping Danger)

If you plan to build on uneven ground, leveling will add time to the construction project. Leveling the ground could end up being a more laborious job than the actual assembly of the play set.

The best location for a play set is level ground; however, absolute level ground will not be the case for many home owners. There may be a slope in the location where you want to place the play set.

If the ground requires leveling, you need to determine how much; the more out of level it is, the more you will need to dig out.

If too much digging is required... you might want to hire an excavator. Most landscapers have the right equipment and are a good place to start getting bids to get your ground leveled.

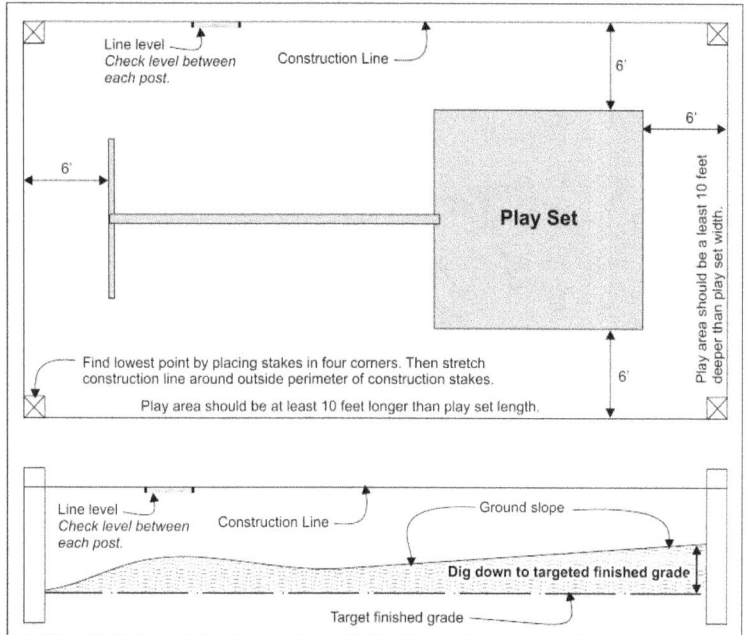

Best play set location in the yard...

This is a personal preference; however, you definitely need to take a few things into consideration:

- Are there any overhead power lines?
- Are there any sharp landscaping objects nearby?
- Is it near a garden bed? (kids will be kids)

Assembly

Any time you do a job like this, organization is very important. Separate everything; however, *DO NOT* open bags of hardware because they are usually bagged in the order of assembly.

If you open all the hardware bags out of sequence, you will have a hard time choosing the correct pieces as you build.

Do you have enough helpers?

Raising parts of a play set can be dangerous. The people who help you need to be prepared, for what they will be expected to do. Take the time to review the installation with your helpers as the job progresses.

Typical parts and hardware for a small play set:

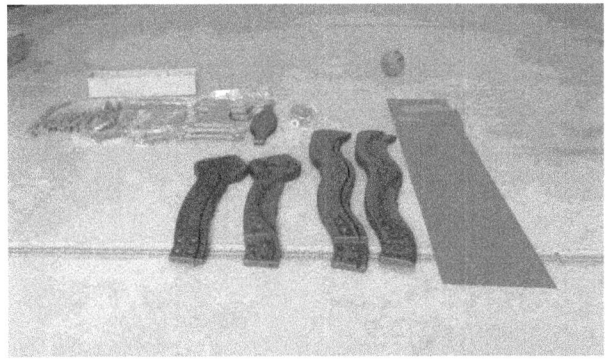

Fitness Equipment

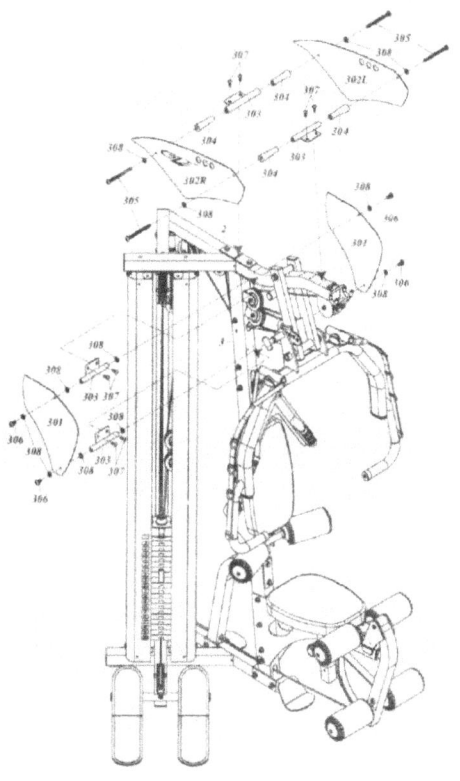

BODYCRAFT GL Training System

Fitness Equipment

Out of all the products that require assembly...

F*itness equipment* is not as labor intensive; however, it is probably the most complicated assembly, since it has mechanical movements, even someone with a higher than average mechanical aptitude may have a hard time understanding how things go together.

A difficult assembly is why you should take pictures whenever possible. Most instructions may be well drafted by the manufacturer; however, a certain level of mechanical aptitude may be needed to follow the instructions.

But all is not lost... you still should be able to assemble any piece of fitness equipment if you know it is going to take some time. If you follow "all" the suggestions laid out in this book and the manufacturer's instructions... you will do fine.

Tools... *if you don't have the right tools and find you have to buy them just to complete the assembly of a piece of fitness equipment, consider this... you might want to hire a professional.*

UnitedAssemblers.com

Minimal tools needed for fitness equipment assembly

- Rubber mallet
- Hammer
- Drill
- Socket set
- Crescent wrenches
- Open & box end wrenches
- Screwdrivers (Phillips & Common)
- Allen (or hex) wrenches (SAE & metric)

The following suggestion cannot be overstated... unless you have assembled any piece of fitness equipment enough times that you could do it in your sleep... you should always *READ THE MANUFACTURERS INSTRUCTIONS!!!*

There are many manufacturers and although the designs are different, the assemblies are basically the same.

Knowing all the different systems and their process to assemble them efficiently will take experience; however, the actual assemblies are basically the same, and taking your time should prove to give you great end results.

Assembly

Before getting started, be sure to read and understand the chapters *"Getting started page 13 & Understanding the instructions page 17"*.

Even though there is a higher level of complexity, assembling fitness equipment can be assembled by anyone with the tools and patience, if you understand this book and read the manufacturer's instructions you shouldn't have any problems. It might just take some time to get it done.

Don't forget to organize all the parts, hardware and discard the trash before you get started.

If possible, more than any other piece of ready to assemble product, you should take as many pictures as you can at a local store (if available) to help you where the instructions may seem a little ambiguous.

Photos of a sample of a small gym system:

As you can see in each photo, the parts are laid out for easy access.

More fitness equipment photos for same product:

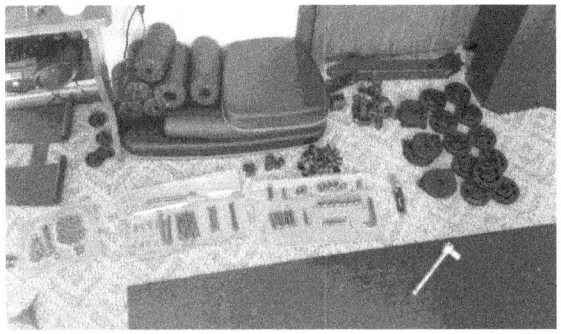

Furniture

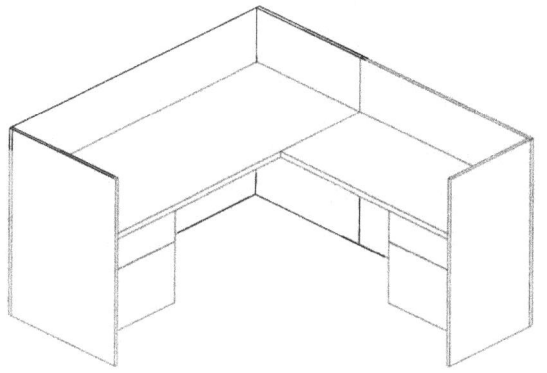

Furniture

Of all assembly projects, furniture assembly is probably the least labor intensive and easiest to assemble.

Tools... *it doesn't take too many special tools to complete almost any furniture assembly project, but consider this is you know you don't have much patience when it comes to these types of tasks... you might want to hire a professional.*

UnitedAssemblers.com

Minimal tools needed to assemble furniture:

- Hammer
- Impact drill (optional)
- Screwdrivers (Phillips & Common)
- Utility knife

Furniture manufacturers usually include tools to assemble their products. However, the quality of those tools may not provide you with what it takes to do the job most efficiently.

Again... this suggestion cannot be overstated... unless you have assembled enough furniture that you could do it in your sleep... you should always *READ THE MANUFACTURER'S INSTRUCTIONS!!!*

The main problem you will encounter with furniture assembly is not paying attention to which hardware goes where. For example: there may be screws that look alike, however, the slightest difference could be the length of a screw and sometimes, those screws may have no immediate visible difference. If you use a screw that is slightly too long in an area that calls for a shorter screw... you may find an unwanted hole with the extra-long screw sticking out of a finished side.

In addition, some of the other products I mention in this book can be assembled out of sequence, if you know what you're doing. When it comes to furniture... if the sequence is assembled in the wrong order, you will most likely have to take it apart and reassemble it.

Any time you discover a piece is in the wrong place, and you have to take the furniture apart, there's a good chance something is going to break or strip out when you make the attempt.

There are many manufacturers, and the assembly of any product is designed in different ways, but most of them use similar hardware.

Below is a photo of all the parts to a lateral file:

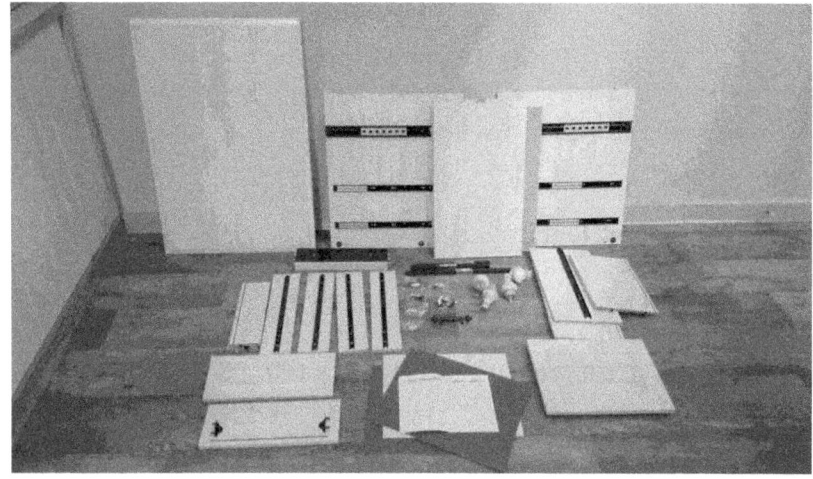

**Quality comes from those
who take pride in their work.**

Quality Products (Better Results)

When purchasing ready to assemble products, you need to consider buying quality.

If not done correctly, quality products can be assembled in such a way that they will not be worth the money you paid for them.

But then on the other hand, a cheap product, if assembled correctly, could be worth more than what you paid for it, but that will be the result of a quality assembly job.

Whenever you buy a product that requires assembly; you really do want to make sure that you take the time and have the confidence to assemble it correctly. If you don't have the tools, time or patience, you should hire a professional assembly technician.

Before you purchase a product that requires assembly, do a little research on the Internet and read the reviews by customers who have already purchased the product.

Remember, it doesn't matter if you decide to do the assembly yourself or if you plan to hire a professional; the end result of any assembled product will almost always have two factors in them...

1. The quality of the product.
2. The attention to detail when it comes to assembly.

While there may be exceptions when it comes to the price of a product, one thing is for sure, the quality put into the actual assembly of the product cannot be compromised.

When it comes to hiring someone for an assembly job... you really do get what you pay for.

UnitedAssemblers.com

Hardware

Hardware

Knowledge of typical hardware and the basic mechanics of them will help you excel at assembling any product.

In this chapter, you will see the fundamentals for hardware through photographs and descriptions. For actual use of the listed hardware and more, go to **YouTube.com/TheSavvyTech**.

Your knowledge of tools for a particular piece of hardware is very important; you should always know the correct tool to use with which hardware. Using the wrong tools could damage the hardware, the product, or worse, cause an injury.

A fastener is a piece of hardware used to mechanically join or affix two or more objects together. How and why hardware/fasteners are used is a very important part of the assembly. Knowing how to use them and which ones are to be used will determine the ultimate success of your assembly job.

Using the wrong fastener in the wrong place can damage the product. The best way to avoid this is to read and study the instructions.

The more familiar you are with the hardware and the tools required to be used on them, the easier and faster your assembly project will go.

There is a large assortment of hardware available; trying to cover all of them in this chapter would be impossible. What has been covered is a typical collection of what you will most likely see in assembly applications.

The next chapter is a glossary with definitions of the hardware's typical use. Using the correct hardware in the right places will definitely affect the success of your assembly job.

There are a few manufacturers that don't put a lot of thought into the hardware they use. It could be from an inexperienced engineer or worse, just a way to cuts costs in the hardware itself.

Something most "professional" technicians carry with them at all times is an extra collection of the typical hardware used for the most common things they assemble on a daily basis.

It is a good idea for the professional assembly technician to be prepared for missing or broken hardware. This can lead to one or more trips to the hardware store; resulting in frustration.

When an assembly technician is prepared and has a supply of typical hardware, the job will be less stressful and the consumer will look upon that technician as a professional.

If you are replacing anything beyond the typical hardware items that may have been designed specifically for the product being assembled, you can call the manufacturer and request whatever you need, to complete the project.

When retrofitting or replacing the manufacturer's hardware with standard hardware that you can buy at the local hardware store or home center, you will need to be careful doing so, since you need to know if, for example, the thread is a standard or metric, or right or left handed threads.

The difference between standard or special hardware can be the hardness or softness of the hardware itself.

Typically, the harder the material of the hardware the more expensive it is. However, it is important that you replace hardware with a specified hardness since that particular part of the product may be designed for a specific stress factor.

When it comes to securing heavy items in an area that will be under a lot of stress, the harder the grade of hardware the better.

Mechanical fasteners (glossary of typical hardware)

There is an entire universe of hardware/fasteners. However, what you have in this chapter is the hardware most used with RTA products.

The following is a quick list of typical nuts used in assembly of products.

Nuts

1	2	3	4	5	6

1 - **Standard nuts** are almost always used with some type of washer.

2 – **Nylon locking nuts** have multiple uses. It can be used in place of a locking washer and standard nut; or it can be used to snug up to parts that may need to have a little movement, where the nut will not back off.

3 – **Flange nuts** has ridges on the bottom side of the nut, allowing it to bite into the material being fastened, which help keep the nut from spinning while the bolt is being tightened it also allows the assembly to be tightened without over-torqueing.

4 – **Cap nuts** can be a decorative cover or a way to prevent someone from getting cut by the threads that normally protrude out of a "standard" nut.

5 – **Wing nuts** are used to allow tightening of parts by hand, without the torqueing needed for a more secure application.

6 – **Barrel nuts** (actually specialty hardware) provide a better connection for wood when the end of one piece is attached to another.

Bolts

The following is a quick list of typical bolts used in assembly of products.

1	2	3	4	5	6

1 – **Typical bolts** are used in a wide variety of applications, especially where load-carrying capacity is a requirement and a typical screw will not adequately be considered a secure method. Through bolting is always the best when possible.

2 – **Machine screws** are used when a strong connection is required and needs to be recessed below the connecting surface.

3 – **Button head machine screws** are typically used to provide a certain amount of safety, which prevents the screw from catching, or injuring, but in many cases is used to give a finished look.

4 – **Carriage bolts** have a few basic uses. (1) To allow the bolt to move in a channel to provide adjustments to whatever is being fastened. (2) To allow hard-to-reach places to provide bolting of objects without the use of a tool on the end with the head of the bolt. (3) To give the product a finished look.

5 – **Lag bolts** (are actually screws) are acceptable for securing something that only requires shear fastening and where there is no actual pulling on the threads. They can be considered self-tapping; however, a pilot hole drilled before use is advised to prevent splitting. Whenever possible, a machine bolt should always be used. Lag bolts of any kind are typically used to cut cost and installation time.

6 – **Machined eye bolts** are used where extra holding power is needed, to prevent the fastener from being pulled out. A good example of its use would be for the attachment of swings on a play set where there is more pulling than sheer force.

Screws

The following is a quick list of typical screws used in assembly of products.

1	2	3	4	5	6

1 – **Typical wood screws** are a piece of hardware with many uses. Whenever possible, a wood screw should have a minimum gripping length two thirds more than the thickness of the material being fastened to.

2 – **Button head screws** are typically used where a greater holding power is needed, where a thin piece is being fastened as to not allow the head of the screw to pass through, tearing out the pilot hole.

3 – **Double ended screws** are typically used to attach a decorative item so the screw is hidden. A common place where these screws are used is for attaching decorative wooden feet to a piece of furniture.

4 – **Self tapping screws** are used to drill a hole and at the same time allowing the screw threads to grip the hole as it is being drilled; thus eliminating the need to drill a pilot hole before using a screw. This type of screw is typically used where sheet goods are being fastened to something else.

5 – **Set screws** are typically used to prevent movement. For example: to prevent a pulley from spinning on a shaft.

6 – **Lag style eye bolts** are used in areas where there is more sheer force than pulling force. Whenever possible, a machine eye bolt should always be used. Lag bolts of any kind are typically used to cut cost and installation time.

Washers

The following is a quick list of typical washers used in assembly of products.

A washer is a thin, flat ring that may be made of metal, plastic, or rubber and depending on the type of washer, can have many uses.

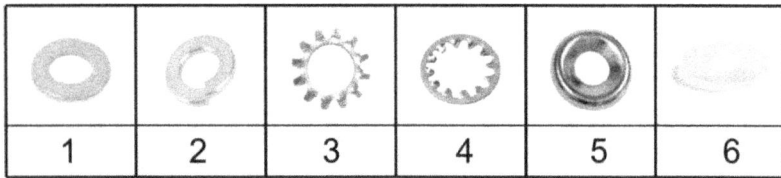

1	2	3	4	5	6

1 – **Standard washers** are typically used to prevent a nut, bolt or both from marring a surface. For wood applications, a washer helps prevent a nut or bold from being pulled through during tightening or wear. A standard washer may also be used to cover oversize holes for the allowance of a little movement between the parts for proper alignment.

2 – **Split washers** are typically used for locking purposes, preventing nuts or bolts from backing off.

3 – **Outside star washers** are also used for locking purposes but have a better distribution of locking power than a split washer.

4 – **Inside star washer** has the same properties as the outside washer.

5 – **Countersink washers** are typically used for decorative applications where a standard wood screw is used.

6 – **Nylon or plastic washers** are typically used to allow parts to move without marring the surfaces of whatever is being fastened together.

Specialty

The following is a quick list of some miscellaneous hardware used in assembly of products.

1	2	3	4	5	6

1 - **T-nuts** are typically used in soft materials like wood or plastic for construction of furniture, play sets and other similar applications. It allows for a greater gripping power where through bolting is not possible or desired.

2 - **The spring clip**, also known as a u-nut is typically used in assemblies for attaching thin materials. It can be machine threaded or split.

3 - **Connector nuts & bolts** are typically used in cabinetry. Their use is to provide a strong connection without the visibility from the head of a nut or bolt.

4 - **Knockdown fasteners** have a few other names depending on the manufacturer. It is typically used in ready to assemble furniture applications.

5 - **Dowel pins and cam locks** are also typically used for ready to assemble furniture applications.

6 - **Threaded inserts** are typically used in wood or plastic, to allow the use of a machine screw or bolt, by giving the application a stronger gripping power where through bolting is not possible or desired.

Treadmill Repair

Treadmill Repair (basic diagnostics & fixes)

Let's talk about how to keep your treadmill running so you are too.

This bonus chapter has been prepared for anyone who wants to save some money when it comes time for basic repairs on a treadmill. It is also a very good primer for anyone who is considering the fitness equipment repair business.

All information within this chapter (like all the others) can be used by those who receive it, learn from it and apply it through practical application.

Most of the service calls I received were customers who thought their treadmill had an electrical or motor problem; however, the problem was almost always the walking or motor belt.

Anyone with a little knowledge and guidance can fix most belt issues themselves and save a lot of money.

When it comes to belt issues, the fix-it yourself person may want to hire a professional if the belt requires replacement. To replace a belt requires the treadmill to be taken almost all the way apart.

Most consumers don't know about the need for regular maintenance for their treadmill and rarely (if ever) have it serviced until it breaks down. Belt breakdowns almost always prove to also have damaged electrical or mechanical parts. The reason for this is the belts friction and drag which can cause electronics to overheat and fail.

I have provided fitness equipment service for many years and have found, the most important thing many owners' manuals rarely explain, is the importance of treadmill maintenance.

The walking belt requires occasional lubrication, and by not doing so will eventually cause electrical and mechanical treadmill problems.

There are some manufacturers that claim a new belt design provides maintenance free treadmills. Don't bank on it... "ALL" mechanical parts that move... require maintenance sometime.

Most owners' manuals can easily be found online. All you need to do to find one is a simple search engine inquiry by entering, "owner's manual", then "the make and model" of your treadmill.

Here is what happens when you do not lubricate the belt... as the surfaces on the underside of the belt and the top of the deck are constantly rubbing together, the friction causes drag and places strain on the electronics, including the motor.

Always use a liquid Teflon Silicone lubricant... NEVER use a silicone spray. However, check with the manufacturer about their recommendations.

One last thing... NEVER start your treadmill while standing on the belt. Doing so causes your treadmill to work harder on startup.

NEVER lubricate a motor belt.

Every time I arrived on a service call where the motor failed, the lower control board was burnt-out, or the belt wouldn't stay adjusted correctly, it was because the customer was too heavy for the treadmill.

Yes, there is a problem with someone buying a treadmill with a low horse power motor rating. Count on a problem when someone weighing 275 pounds tries running on a treadmill with only a 1.5 horsepower motor.

The best rule of thumb for weight ratios and the size of treadmill motors to prevent paying high repair fees to get it fixed on a regular basis:

Weight to Horsepower Suggestions

Your Weight	Motor Horsepower
Up to 175 pounds	1.5 HP min
176 to 275 pounds	2.5 HP min
276 to 375 pounds	3.5 HP min
Over 376 pounds	4 HP or larger

Finding & fixing typical belt problems

Treadmill starts, but the belt stops or hesitates when stepped on. There are a few reasons for this to happen:

1. **The treadmill belt**

    If the belt is loose, you can simply tighten it; however, if you over-tighten, it could damage the belt or break the end cap brackets. Use a ruler and raise the belt in the middle of the walking deck to a height of about 2.5 inches.

    If the belt is worn, it will not operate at its peak efficiency. For best performance and extended life of a treadmill, the belt should be replaced.

    Before buying a new walking belt, check to see whether you also need a deck. A cracked deck will wear new belts out and proper adjustment may be impossible.

2. **Broken end cap or brackets**

    This is typically caused by over-tightening the belts adjustment screws. Broken end caps or brackets can also be damaged moving the treadmill from one location to another.

3. **Pulley slipping on front roller**

    Rare, but this problem is typically caused by over-tightening either the motor belt or the walking belt. Typically, this only happens on cheaper treadmills.

4. **Broken or cracked deck**

    Broken decks can be caused by someone too heavy for the treadmill being used.

    A deck can also crack by running on the heal of the foot and not on the ball of the foot. Running on the ball of your foot allows for cushioning for both your joints and the treadmills' deck.

The best way to discover where the belt is slipping is to watch the front roller. *(Remove the cover for best viewing).*

1. Turn the treadmill on
2. Watch the front roller
3. Step on the belt with one foot pressing down to stop it.
   (NEVER STAND ON BELT WHILE STARTING TREADMILL)
4. If the walking belt stops after stepping on it, and the front roller continues to spin, the walking belt is slipping. This is easily fixed by making adjustments near the rear roller. SEE NEXT PAGE

Never turn adjustment screws more than a half turn at a time and be sure to turn equally on both sides. Repeat steps 2-4 until belt stops slipping.

CAUTION - do not over tighten since this can cause other problems. Remember, you should be able to raise the belt 2.5 inches, anything less... the belt is too tight.

If the walking belt stops and the front roller/pulley stops spinning, it is the motor belt slipping. This problem is easily fixed by applying more tension to the motor belt.

NOTE: Most manufacturers have different ways to adjust the tension on the motor belts. Observe the way the motor is mounted and determine the best way to make the tightening adjustment

CAUTION – over-tightening the motor belt will also cause other parts to wear or break. You should not be able to twist the belt more than 90 degrees with your fingers.

Another possibility that is not as common… if the walking belt stops and the front roller also stops spinning… look closely at the pulley attached to the front roller. If the pulley is spinning on the roller, the roller is bad and requires replacement (there is usually a loud screeching sound).

Locating the parts:

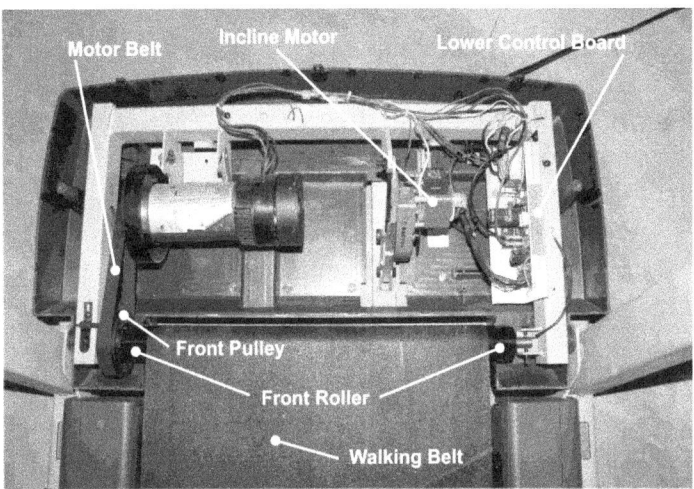

Making adjustments on a slipping belt:

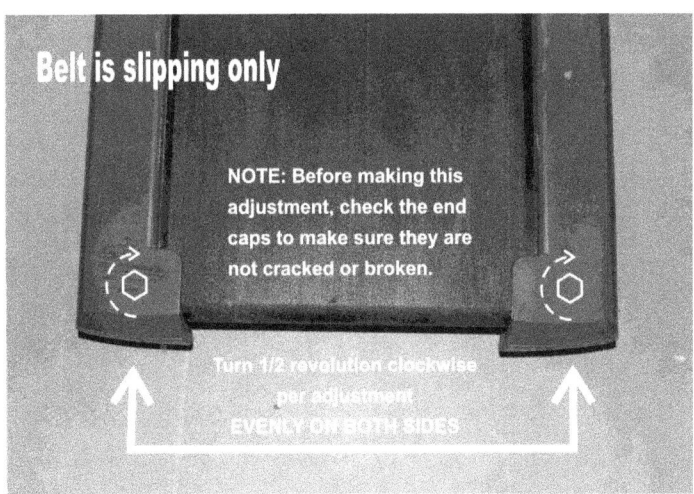

The treadmill belt is tracking and rubbing on one side. There are a few reasons for this to happen:

1. **The belt is improperly adjusted**

   There is a certain amount of patience required to make this adjustment, especially if you are not skilled in how the belt tracks on the deck.

   Turn the treadmill on to its lowest speed and watch the belt. If the belt starts tracking in one direction… tighten the tensioning screw on the side the belt is traveling in by only a half turn. Repeat until belt self-centers and stays. *See images on next page.*

2. **The belt tensioners have been over-tightened causing broken end cap(s)**

   Depending on the style of the end cap or bracket and the condition of the break, you will probably need to replace one or both of them.

3. **The treadmill is not level**

   This is not always a visible problem… a three foot carpenters level is needed to make sure the treadmill is evenly distributed on the floor side-to-side if you are having belt adjustment problems.

Tracking adjustments

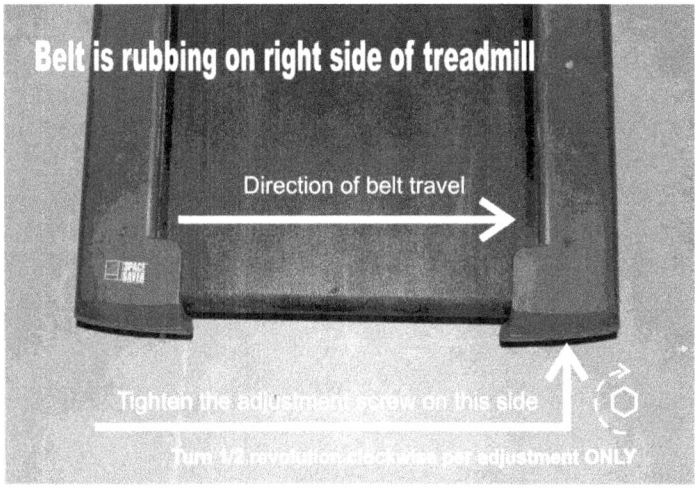

NOTE: for both above and below adjustments, ONLY make half 1/2 turns each time. To fine tune, you may need to make a 1/4 turn.

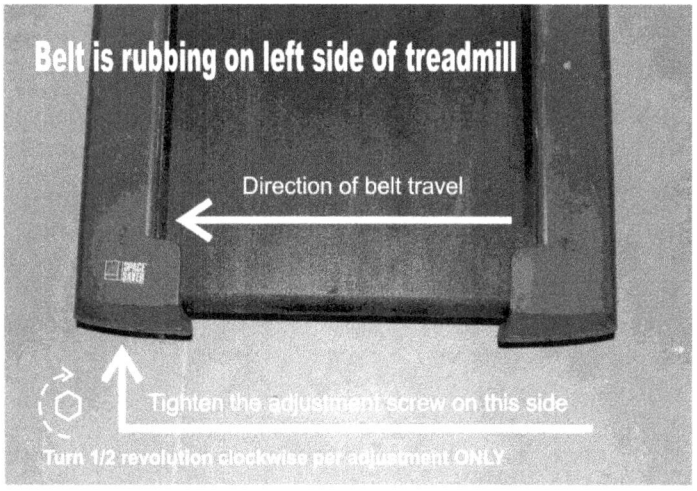

Electronic Problems…

I am not going to get into electrical repairs in this book. If you are having problems beyond the belt, it may be time to hire a professional.

However, with that being said, many electronic problems are caused by an improper power source.

Your treadmill is a heavy duty appliance. It needs the proper connection to keep electronics from overloading.

All treadmills need to be connected to a grounded outlet!

Additionally a ground fault outlet is not an acceptable connection.

I can't tell you how many people have connected their treadmill to a power source that may only be 10 feet away with a 100 foot extension cord with a 16 gauge wire.

If you use an underrated extension cord, you are not only looking at causing the control board on your treadmill to eventually burn out, but it is a critical fire hazard.

There are appliance extension cords; if you can't find one, use an extension cord that is less than 25 feet long and has at least a 12 gauge wire.

If a treadmill is more than 25 feet from the nearest outlet, you should have a licensed electrician install a new outlet or move the treadmill closer to another location that has an outlet within the 25 feet.

Additional problems for a treadmill that causes its electronics to fail;

1. If you don't have your treadmill serviced on a regular basis.
2. Placing the treadmill in a dusty area, like a utility room with a dryer or any other source that creates dust.
3. By not cleaning under your treadmill on a regular basis with a vacuum. The rotation of a treadmill belt creates a vacuum and pulls dirt, dust and other unwanted items into the control compartment, under the motor control cover.

Calibration Sequences:

There are too many makes and models of treadmills to print all of their calibration sequences in this book.

If you think your treadmill needs to be calibrated, check your owners' manual or call the manufacturer. Most manufacturers should be more than happy to help you with calibrations on their products.

If you don't have the owner's manual, most of them can be downloaded from the manufacturer's websites. Just search the make and model of your treadmill using "owner's manual" in the search query.

For example:

Search: *The make the model* "*owner's manual*" of course replace "*make and model*" with whichever make and model you actually have.

UNITED

ASSEMBLERS

Hiring a Professional

I can't tell you how many times I walked into the home of new customer with their greeting being, *"I am so glad I found you, or, I didn't know there were people that actually specialized in this kind of work."*

The assembly and installation industry is a very niche and a highly skilled trade just like a carpenter, electrician, mechanic or plumber. You wouldn't call an electrician to fix a plumbing problem would you?

The opportunity and evolution of this industry has many handy people presenting themselves as being capable of doing this kind of work... many of them cannot.

As people who call themselves handy and make themselves available to do assembly or installation work, they find out quickly that they don't want to deal with complex instructions or diagnose repair problems.

Many assembly or installation jobs can be somewhat of a challenge, especially when the handy person doesn't know how or where to get started; hence, the reason for this book.

BEWARE: There is a certain amount of vulnerability for the consumer; that comes from opportunists who see this type of works a fast and easy way to make money.

Hiring an unskilled individual will almost always provide the unsuspecting consumer with less than desirable results.

All I am saying here is, if you are looking for someone to assemble something for you, consider hiring someone who specializes in what it is that they do and has credentials to prove it.

Independent Professionals

Until the United Assemblers Network (UAN) was founded, there has not been an educational source for the assembly, installation and repair industry. Anyone could say they knew what they were doing and claim they provided professional services.

Through membership, the UAN makes available to rookie as well as veteran technicians, as much information as they want to consume, to make them the pros that they say they are or want to be. As the pros in the UAN gain more knowledge, they pass it on to others within our industry. They do this through monthly conference calls and annual meetings held at a determined venue.

When it comes time to hire someone to assemble, install or repair anything you need serviced, consider a few easy questions for your prospective contractor. They should have quick answers to the following.

Questions to ask a professional:

1. Are you insured?
2. Can you provide a background check?
3. Are you a member of any assembly trade organization?
4. Is your business registered within your state?
5. Do you have any references?

Other things you should consider asking to legitimize the independent contractor:

1. Do they have a website?
2. Do they have business cards?
3. Do they use a professional email address?
4. What is their demeanor on the phone?
5. If you called and got their voicemail message, was it professional? If you left a message, how quick did they get back with you?
6. Did they come to you with a professional work order or invoice for you to sign approving their work?

National Assembly Companies

This could be the best place for someone to break into the business without spending a lot of money in marketing to get started.

National Assembly Companies, or NAC's, as we call them in the industry, are in business because the objective of retailers is to have a one stop shop.

Today retailers sell the service, collect the money, and dispatch the job to a national assembly company. The reason... a retailer's corporate office would rather send out one check, than hundreds of them to independent assembly contractors.

When anyone buys a product from almost any retailer, chances are very high that if they provide the service, the person arriving to your location is almost always <u>NOT</u> an employee of that store. For that reason, NAC's are always looking for people who can provide this type of work professionally.

If you have never done this type of work before, you might want to consider taking the UANCT (United Assemblers Certification Test) to at a minimum show the NAC you are considering to contract with, that you at least know what you are doing.

Make good money

In a very niche industry

Business Opportunity

The United Assemblers Network (UAN) has developed an outstanding opportunity in a very niche market.

Most people have no idea there are people who actually provide the type of services we do (assembly, installation and repair).

We are a skilled trade, but not recognized like a carpenter, mechanic, electrician, plumber or any other "skilled" trade; however, the UAN is changing that.

This is an AWESOME opportunity for the handy person.

Everyone has run across products in a retail store on display; however, when the consumer finds out it requires assembly or installation they haven't known where to turn... until now.

To this day, when anyone doing this kind of work walks into a customer's location, most of those customers to this day still say "WOW"... *I didn't even know there were people out there like you that specialized in this type of work.*

The main reasons our services are needed is the consumer typically doesn't have the tools, time, patience or experience to assemble or install the products they buy in a timely manner or more important, correctly.

As for what someone can earn... there is no ceiling! If you are a self-starter with a high mechanical aptitude... the potential is unlimited.

There are members of our network making six figures a year!!!

The United Assemblers Network (UAN) has an outstanding opportunity for the person that wants to grow their very own lucrative business with a very small investment. Sometimes, hardly any investment at all if the aspiring assembly tech already has the tools.

What the UAN provides

You already have this book which can be an awesome primer for the handyperson with a high mechanical aptitude. There are also:

- How to Videos
- Camaraderie
- Exposure

You also have access to all of the UAN's combined experience (that experience goes into the hundreds of years) through the events we have and the camaraderie of this network as we all share techniques, business building ideas of what works and what does not work so that you have a much... much shorter learning curve.

Where the UAN can give guidance:

- How to do it right
- Marketing
- Website optimization
- Customer service

If you are still wondering, "why the UAN"?

Our network has a very low annual membership fee and since the UAN doesn't get into your pocket for every single job you do... the business owners of our network prosper at least twice as much as technicians who contract with national assembly companies.

With the UAN, you make more money whether it is the exposure through relationships we build with the online dealers, retailers and manufacturers or through your own efforts that you learn here by marketing locally or (*if you want to*) by contracting with one or more of the National Assembly Companies known as the NAC.

By contracting with an NAC, your start up can be successful overnight; but only if the NAC has the volume for you.... the NAC you contract with should also be members of the UAN; if they are not, be very skeptical of their motives.

When you join the UAN... you are in business for yourself but not necessarily by yourself.

We have monthly calls where we share our experiences of things that work and don't work so that other members of our great network don't make the same mistakes.

We have one conference every year where you can meet and greet your brothers and sisters in this awesome new industry as well as manufacturers, retailers and online dealers.

If you are a handy person... we know you're excited about the possibilities... contact the UAN today to jump start your career in a very niche industry.

Have I mentioned yet... I love my job?

About me

My history in the assembly industry all started by accident.

Like many good things, most people don't know when they have something handed to them that could be life changing; and when they do, seldom do anything with it.

I have always loved building and fixing things.

Since I had this in my blood, the assembly industry was an awesome fit that allowed me to help people while actually having fun. Not too many people are blessed with that kind of career.

I also have a background in the *sign industry* as a draftsman and research manager of building codes, to determine permissibility for a business' signage; along with providing a little engineering support.

Along that journey of working at a few commercial sign shops in central Ohio, I made some really good friends… one of them being Chris Manack.

There was a point when I had my own small vinyl sign shop where I made small real estate signs and did some vehicle lettering.

One day, like most other days, things were not all that busy.

I received a phone call from Chris asking me how things were going at the shop.

I said, "Not so good"… Chris replied, "Good"! Perplexed by his response I remember asking… "What does that mean"?

Chris went on to tell me there was some assembly work where he needed a helper. So long story short, the next day, I closed the shop and went with Chris.

At the end of the day of assembling some office furniture with Chris, I asked him if he was hiring. Chris replied no, but the company I contract with is.

It took less than a week and I was on board with the National Assembly Company and cranking out the assemblies. I saw the potential in the assembly industry and started my own small furniture assembly service in Central Ohio.

After a local ready-to-assemble superstore decided they would pass out my assembly business cards; I setup a website called *Assemble-4-You* to help enhance my business cards and other printed advertising.

Around this same time, another national assembly company was looking for a tech in the central Ohio area. When they found my website, I received a phone call from them asking me if I would be interested in contracting with them.

Gracefully I turned them down as a tech; that same national assembly company came back with another offer a couple weeks later to buy my website and hiring me as a regional manager.

The difference between this company and my small local assembly service was, they would assemble, install and repair anything and they had hundreds of technicians that I would be responsible for.

Even though I was a natural at everything they offered, it opened my eyes as to how big this assembly industry really is.

That company eventually failed along with two more of the NAC's I had worked for as a managing employee.

So another long story short... I became an expert in this industry of all of the products we serviced as a technician and a corporate training manager.

I took my training position very serious and bought a video camera to record training sessions so aspiring technicians I recruited from around the country could get up to par quickly.

Today, I have experience on both sides of the proverbial fence as a corporate manager and a lifelong technician. You see, I always have been and always will be a technician first.